BRITANNICA BEGINNER BIOS

MALALA YOUSAFZAI

NOBEL PEACE PRIZE–WINNING CHAMPION OF FEMALE EDUCATION

HEATHER MOORE NIVER

Britannica®
Educational Publishing

IN ASSOCIATION WITH

ROSEN
EDUCATIONAL SERVICES

Published in 2016 by Britannica Educational Publishing (a trademark of Encyclopædia Britannica, Inc.) in association with The Rosen Publishing Group, Inc.
29 East 21st Street, New York, NY 10010

Distributed exclusively by Rosen Publishing.
To see additional Britannica Educational Publishing titles, go to rosenpublishing.com.

First Edition

Britannica Educational Publishing
J.E. Luebering: Director, Core Reference Group
Mary Rose McCudden: Editor, Britannica Student Encyclopedia

Rosen Publishing
Amelie von Zumbusch: Editor
Nelson Sá: Art Director
Nicole Russo : Designer
Cindy Reiman: Photography Manager
Karen Huang: Photo Researcher

Library of Congress Cataloging-in-Publication Data

Niver, Heather Moore.
 Malala Yousafzai / Heather Moore Niver. — First Edition.
     pages cm. — (Britannica Beginner Bios)
 Includes bibliographical references and index.
 Audience: Grades: 1-4.
 ISBN 978-1-68048-253-9 (Library bound) — ISBN 978-1-5081-0058-4 (Paperback) — ISBN 978-1-68048-311-6 (6-pack)
 1. Yousafzai, Malala, 1997-—Juvenile literature. 2. Girls—Education—Pakistan—Juvenile literature. 3. Girls—Violence against—Pakistan—Juvenile literature. 4. Women social reformers—Pakistan—Biography—Juvenile literature. 5. Taliban—Juvenile literature. 6. Pakistan—Social conditions—Juvenile literature. I. Title.
 LC2330.N58 2016
 371.822095491—dc23

2015016641

Manufactured in the United States of America

CONTENTS

CHAPTER ONE

STRONG TEEN ACTIVIST

Malala Yousafzai is a young Pakistani **ACTIVIST**. In many ways she is a regular teenager who likes playing sports, dancing with her friends, and reading books. However, her courage and strength have also made millions of people around the

Vocabulary Box

An **ACTIVIST** is a person who pushes for social or political change.

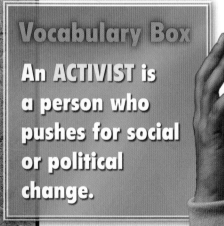

Malala Yousafzai likes to dance and read, but she also travels around the world speaking up for girls' rights.

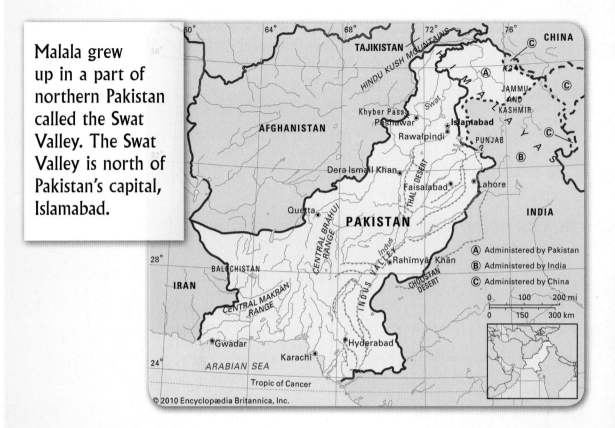

Malala grew up in a part of northern Pakistan called the Swat Valley. The Swat Valley is north of Pakistan's capital, Islamabad.

world look up to her.

The Yousafzai family is Pashtun. The Pashtuns are an ethnic group who live mostly in Pakistan and Afghanistan. Malala grew up in a part of Pakistan called the Swat Valley. The Swat Valley was a beautiful district and a popular vacation destination.

Malala Yousafzai is named after the Pashtun hero Malalai of Maiwand. Malalai helped her people fight against the British in the Battle of Maiwand, during the Second Anglo-Afghan War (1878–80).

This painting shows the Battle of Maiwand. It was at this 1880 battle that Malalai of Maiwand inspired Pashtun soldiers to fight on.

Malala was raised by parents who encouraged her to speak up for what she believes. In 2008 she began to protest the closing of girls' schools in her area. She even wrote a **BLOG** about her experiences and opinions about the limits of women's education.

Vocabulary Box

A **BLOG** is a website on which an author shares his or her personal thoughts.

On October 11, 2013, Malala met with President Barack Obama and his family.

In 2012, when she was only 15 years old, Malala was shot as a result of her activism. She survived the shooting and fully recovered from her injuries. She now speaks all over the world about the importance of the education of girls.

CHAPTER TWO

YOUNG YOUSAFZAI

Ziauddin Yousafzai, Malala's father, is an outspoken social activist, poet, and educator. Her mother, Tor Pekai, is quiet but supports her family with advice. She recently learned how to read and write. Malala's parents married for love, which was unusual. Their families were not happy because Pashtun families normally pick whom their children will marry.

In Malala's CULTURE, baby boys are prized over girls. This is because boys can grow up to sup-

> **Vocabulary Box**
>
> A CULTURE is a pattern of behavior shared by a society, or group of people.

Malala is close to her family. Together, they have shared tragedy and triumph.

Quick Fact

Malala is the oldest of three children. She has two younger brothers. Their names are Khushal and Atal.

port their families. Malala wrote, "I was a girl in a land where rifles are fired in celebration of a son, while daughters are

Pashtun men have traditionally valued boys more highly than girls. Malala's father disagreed.

hidden away…their role in life simply to prepare food and give birth to children." But Ziauddin Yousafzai was proud of his daughter from the first second he saw her. He celebrated Malala's birth and encouraged others to celebrate, too. He also encouraged girls to get an education.

Malala attended the Khushal Girls High School and College. She was a top student there.

Ziauddin Yousafzai ran the Khushal Girls High School and College. Malala became one of the top students there. Her father said, "She was always in the school and always very curious." He always told Malala that she should speak out for what she believed. He encouraged her to learn and read her stories and poems.

Ziauddin Yousafzai always encouraged his daughter to stand up for what she believed in.

Quick Fact

Growing up in Pakistan was tough. When she was 14, Malala said, "Sometimes I think it's easier to be a *Twilight* vampire than a girl in Swat."

When Malala was only 11 years old, she started to speak out about education for girls. But she was still a normal child, too. She enjoyed reading books and watching television.

CHAPTER THREE

LIFE UNDER THE TALIBAN

When Malala was young, her town, Mingora, was a pleasant place to live. They held festivals there every summer. People traveled there to vacation and ski. But everything changed in 2007 when the Taliban invaded the Swat Valley. The Taliban is a group that believes in strict Islamic law. The group had ruled

When the Taliban settled near the Swat Valley, their strict laws changed everything.

Afghanistan from 1996 until 2001 and continued to be powerful in the region. They did not want people to watch movies or television, to dance, or to listen to CDs. Eventually, the Taliban cut off cable television to the whole valley.

The Taliban had very strict rules about women. They did not allow women to participate in everyday society. Women could not go to market to shop. If they went out at all, they had to be completely covered in a **BURKA**. The Taliban made it hard for girls to get an education. They began closing and even blowing up schools for girls.

The Taliban required women to wear burkas to go out in public.

Vocabulary Box

A BURKA is a loose outfit that covers the body from head to toe.

The Taliban invasion brought much violence to the region. There were armed soldiers and helicopters. The Taliban bombed areas of the country. When it became too dangerous to stay, Malala and her family escaped. However, they returned when the violence eased. It was a scary time, and even brave Malala had nightmares.

The people of Swat suffered bombings and other violence because of the Taliban.

Quick Fact

Malala gave her first speech in 2008. It was called "How Dare the Taliban Take Away My Basic Right to Education?" People all over Pakistan heard about it.

By the end of 2008 the Taliban had destroyed 400 schools. In January 2009 all girls' schools were closed. After that, Malala knew she had to speak out. She wrote, "They cannot stop me. I will get my education if it's at home, school or somewhere else. This is our request to all the world—Save our schools. Save our world. Save our Pakistan. Save our Swat."

Malala is a great believer in standing up for what is right. She has said, "When the situation is that terrible, there is no choice but to speak out."

CHAPTER FOUR

"WHO IS MALALA?"

After the Taliban made it illegal for any girl to go to school, Malala Yousafzai began writing about her daily life living under the Taliban. Her **ANONYMOUS** articles were published on a blog for the British Broadcasting Corporation (BBC). Many people all over the world read the BBC blog. In the blog, she described how scared she felt living under the Taliban.

> **Vocabulary Box**
>
> **ANONYMOUS** means not named or identified.

In 2009 Malala was featured in two documentaries about the school shutdown and her experiences. The short films were posted on the *New York Times* website. She was interviewed on television, too. In one interview

Malala's blog got people around the world to pay attention to what was happening in Swat.

she said, "They can stop me going to school but they can't stop me learning." Soon the world figured out who was writing the blog. In 2009

Quick Fact

Malala recited her blog to a reporter using a secret telephone line that could not be traced.

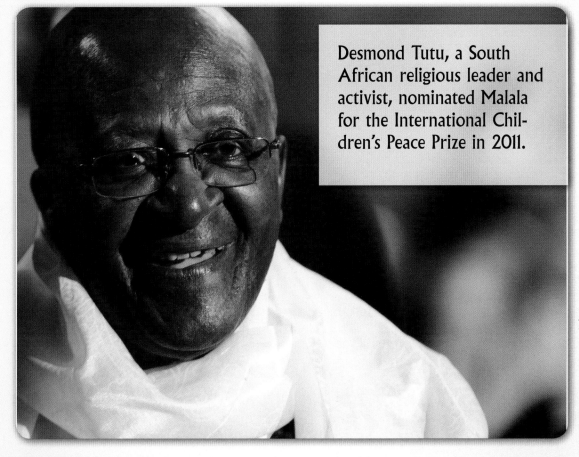

Desmond Tutu, a South African religious leader and activist, nominated Malala for the International Children's Peace Prize in 2011.

the Taliban changed its rules and allowed girls to return to school.

In 2011 Malala began to receive awards for her work. In December she was awarded Pakistan's first National Youth Peace Prize. The prize was later renamed the

Quick Fact

Two of Malala's friends on the bus were also wounded when Malala was attacked.

National Malala Peace Prize. Even though she received awards, her actions continued to put her in danger. Malala and her father both received death threats.

On October 9, 2012, while Malala was on her way home from school, a Taliban gunman came up to her bus. He asked, "Who is Malala?" Before she could answer, she was shot in the head. She survived the attempted ASSASSINATION but was badly hurt. After an operation at a Pakistani hospital, Malala was flown to Birmingham, England, for further treatment. She had to have several more opera-

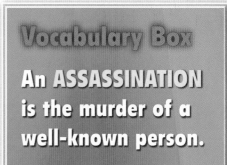

Vocabulary Box

An ASSASSINATION is the murder of a well-known person.

Malala's family supported her while she recovered from the assassination attempt.

tions. The bullet missed her brain, though, so she was able to recover over time. In March 2013 she was ready to return to school. Malala and her family remained in Birmingham because it was too dangerous to return to Pakistan.

CHAPTER FIVE

ONE GIRL AMONG MANY

After the assassination attempt, many powerful people took up Malala's cause. This resulted in Pakistan's first Right to Education bill. The Pakistani president also launched a $10 million education fund in Yousafzai's honor. Around the same time, the Malala Fund was established. This fund supports education for all girls around the world. After Malala's full recovery she continued to travel all over the world to promote the right of every child to an education.

In 2013 Malala won the United Nations

Vocabulary Box

To be INFLUENTIAL means to have the power to cause changes.

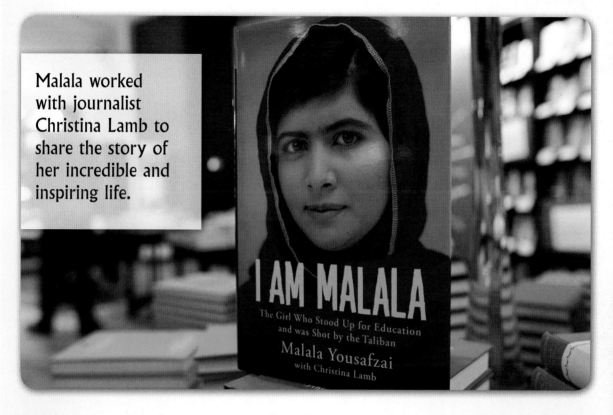

Malala worked with journalist Christina Lamb to share the story of her incredible and inspiring life.

Human Rights Prize. This honor is given out every five years. She was also named one of *Time* magazine's most INFLUENTIAL people in 2013. Around that same time Malala wrote a memoir with the help of the British journalist Christina Lamb. The book was published in 2013. It was called *I Am Malala: The Girl Who Stood Up for Education and Was Shot by the Taliban*.

In 2014 Malala and Kailash Satyarthi were awarded the Nobel Peace Prize.

Malala was nominated for the Nobel Peace Prize in 2013. In 2014 she won the award. She became the youngest person to ever receive the Nobel Peace Prize. She shared the award with Kailash Satyarthi, a children's rights activist from India.

Malala was awarded the World's Children's Prize in 2014. She gave the $50,000 from the award to the United Nations Relief and Works Agency for Palestine. The agency used it to rebuild schools that had been destroyed. As Malala explained, "We must all work to ensure Palestinian boys and girls, and all children everywhere, receive a quality education in a safe

The U.N. Relief and Works Agency helped support this Palestinian school.

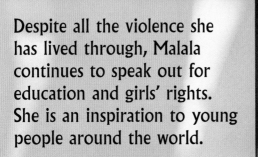

Despite all the violence she has lived through, Malala continues to speak out for education and girls' rights. She is an inspiration to young people around the world.

environment. Because without education, there will never be peace."

A full-length movie about Malala, called *He Named Me Malala*, was released in October 2015. Malala continues to be committed to helping others and promoting education through the Malala Fund. As she said in her now-famous speech to the United Nations Youth Assembly on July 12, 2013, "Here I stand, one girl among many… I raise up my voice… so that those without a voice can be heard."

TIMELINE

1997: Malala Yousafzai is born in Mingora, in Pakistan's Swat Valley, on July 12.

2007: The Swat Valley, once a vacation destination, is invaded by the Taliban.

2008: On September 1, 11-year-old Malala goes with her father to a local press club in Peshawar to protest school closings. She gives her first speech, "How Dare the Taliban Take Away My Basic Right to Education?"

2009: Malala begins writing an anonymous blog for the British Broadcasting Corporation (BBC) in January.

The Taliban closes all girls' schools in Swat on January 15.

Malala makes her first television appearance in February.

Also in February, *New York Times* reporter Adam Ellick works with Malala to make a documentary, *Class Dismissed*, a 13-minute piece about the school shutdown.

Ellick's second short film with Malala, *A Schoolgirl's Odyssey*, appears in October.

2012: Malala is shot on her way home from school on October 9.

The Malala Fund is established on November 10.

2013: Malala is named one of *Time* magazine's most influential people of the year on April 18.

On July 12, her 16th birthday, Malala makes a public appearance for the first time since being shot and addresses an audience of 500 at the United Nations in New York City.

The book that Malala wrote with Christina Lamb, *I Am Malala: The Girl Who Stood Up for Education and Was Shot by the Taliban*, is published on October 8.

Malala is awarded the European Parliament's Sakharov Prize for Freedom of Thought in November.

Malala is awarded the United Nations Human Rights Prize on December 10.

2014: In July, Malala meets with Nigerian president Goodluck Jonathan to discuss efforts to free hundreds of schoolgirls who were kidnapped by the militant group Boko Haram.

On October 21, Malala becomes the youngest person to be awarded the Liberty Medal. The medal is awarded to public figures striving for people's freedom throughout the world.

Malala is awarded the Nobel Peace Prize on December 10. She becomes the youngest recipient in the history of the prize.

2015: In April Malala has an asteroid named after her by a National Aeronautics and Space Administration (NASA) astronomer.

The movie *He Named Me Malala* is released in October.

GLOSSARY

ASTEROID A small, rocky body that circles around the sun.

DOCUMENTARY A movie that presents actual events or facts about something.

ETHNIC GROUP A group of people with common traits and customs and a sense of shared identity.

FUND Money set aside for a special purpose.

INVADE To enter a place to take it over.

JOURNALIST An editor of or writer for a newspaper, a magazine, or radio and television news.

MEMOIR A story of a personal experience.

NOBEL PEACE PRIZE An annual prize that is awarded to people for important work in helping to bring about peace in the world.

NOMINATED Chosen as a candidate for election, appointment, or honor.

OPERATION A procedure performed on a living body, usually with medical instruments, to restore health or repair damage.

SOCIAL Having to do with society, or the life of communities.

TALIBAN A group, based in Afghanistan, that enforces strict Islamic law.

BOOKS

Abouraya, Karen Leggett. *Malala Yousafzai: Warrior with Words*. Great Neck, NY: StarWalk Kids Media, 2014.

Doak, Robin S. *Malala Yousafzai* (True Books). New York, NY: Children's Press/F. Watts Trade, 2015.

Hansen, Grace. *Malala Yousafzai: Education Activist* (History Maker Biographies). Minneapolis, MN: Abdo Kids, 2015.

Small, Kathleen. *Malala Yousafzai: Teenage Education Activist who Defied the Taliban*. New York, NY: Cavendish Square, 2014.

WEBSITES

Because of the changing nature of Internet links, Rosen Publishing has developed an online list of websites related to the subject of this book. This site is updated regularly. Please use this link to access the list:

http://www.rosenlinks.com/BBB/You

INDEX